Be a
History
Detective

Victorian Transport

Liz Gogerly

WAYLAND

This book is a differentiated text version of
The History Detective Investigates Victorian Transport
by Colin Stott

This edition first published in 2009 by Wayland.

Copyright © Wayland 2009

Wayland
Hachette Children's Books
338 Euston Road
London NW1 3BH

Wayland Australia
Level 17/207 Kent Street
Sydney NSW 2000

Commissioning Editor: Jennifer Sanderson
Designer: Elaine Wilkinson
Proofreader: Hayley Fairhead
Cartoon Artwork: Richard Hook
Picture Research: Shelly Noronha

British Library Cataloguing in Publication Data:
   Gogerly, Liz
   Victorian transport. - Differentiated ed. -
   (Be a history detective)
   1. Transportation - Great Britain -
   History - 19th century
   - Juvenile literature 2. Great Britain - Social life
   and customs - 19th century - Juvenile literature
   I. Title II. Stott, Colin
   388'.0941'09034

ISBN: 978 0 7502 5708 4

Printed in China

Wayland is a division of
Hachette Children's Books,
an Hachette UK Company.
www.hachette.co.uk

Picture acknowledgements:

The Publishers would like to thank the following for permission to reproduce their pictures: Bridgeman Art Library 4, 7 (top), 11 (bottom), 17 (bottom), 22 (top); Hulton Getty 24 (bottom), 25; Mary Evans Picture Library 6, 7 (bottom), 10, 11 (top), 13 (bottom), 15 (bottom), 19, 22 (bottom), 23, 24 (top), 28; Public Record Office 27; Science & Society cover (Great Eastern and Pullman Car), 1, 5, 8 (bottom), 9 (top), 13 (top), 15 (top), 18 (both), 19, 26, 27 (bottom), 29 (bottom); Wayland Picture Library cover (Broad Gauge, Merryweather Engine and canal), 8, 9 (bottom), 12, 14, 16, 17 (top) 20 (both), 21, 29 (top).

Note:
The website addresses included in this book were valid at the time of going to press. However, because of the nature of the Internet, it is possible that some addresses may have changed, or sites may have changed or closed down since publication. While the authors and Publishers regret any inconvenience this may cause the readers, no responsibility for any such changes can be accepted by either the author or the Publishers.

Contents

Words in **bold** can be found
in the glossary.

Travel in Victorian times

Queen Victoria ruled Britain from 1837 until 1901. Victorian Britain was a powerful country. Queen Victoria ruled a large **empire**. Britain lead the world in trade and industry.

Quicker and cheaper travel

Life in Britain changed a lot in Victorian times. Many new ideas and inventions were discovered. There were enormous changes to transport and travel. In the 1830s, travel was expensive and slow. Most people did not travel far from home. Farmers and **manufacturers** usually supplied only local areas. By 1901, transport was cheaper, faster and more reliable.

The history detective

Sherlock Bones is the history detective. He will help you to find out about Victorian transport. Follow the clues and learn how people travelled in Victorian times.

Whenever you see one of Sherlock's paw-prints there is a mystery for you to solve. See pages 30 and 31 for the answers.

Detective work

Visit your school library or your local library to look for books about Queen Victoria and the Victorians. Start to collect background information about the Victorians.

"If we had to sum up our age… it is 'the mechanical age'. There is no end to machinery. We fight with simple nature and, with our unbeatable engines, always win and prosper."

Great Exhibition Catalogue, 1871

❧ How many different ways of travelling can you see on this page?

Horses and wagons

Horses were an important way of travelling in Victorian times. When other forms of transport were discovered, horses were still used by most people. Horses were used for many different jobs too.

Horse and coaches

Rich people had their own horses and coaches. Poorer people walked everywhere. Stagecoaches were the main way of travelling long distances. Travel by stagecoach took a long time. The coaches were overcrowded and uncomfortable. There were lots of stops at roadside inns for fresh horses and food. Sometimes travellers stayed overnight at an inn.

❖ How many people can you see in the stagecoach in the picture?

▼ *Tickets for the stagecoach were expensive.*

◀ *Water carts were used to clean roads.*

Detective work

Find out how horses were used in Victorian Britain. Local museums may have photographs. You could contact local shops and businesses that were opened in Victorian times.

Carrier wagons

Poor people could not afford to travel by stagecoach. Instead, they bought rides on carrier wagons. These wagons were used to carry heavy goods. Teams of horses pulled the wagons along. The wagons had wide wheels and travelled very slowly.

Horse power

In cities, horses were used to pull hackney carriages or hansom cabs. These were like taxi cabs. In towns and in the countryside, horses and carts were used for deliveries.

Lady Charlotte Bonham Carter, said:

"...with all the horse traffic, there was an awful amount of dirt on the streets."

▶ *A horse-drawn hansom cab.*

Early river boats

In early Victorian times, boats were important for industry. The rivers and **canals** of Britain were filled with boats carrying heavy goods. Many parts of the country had their own type of boat. For example, in East Anglia, there were **barge**s with sails. These were called wherries and they carried farm goods.

The canals

Heavy goods were transported along canals on barges and narrow boats. Until the 1880s, horses were used to pull the boats. The horses walked along a path next to the water. Later, most boats were fitted with steam engines.

▲ **Locks** on the Regent's Canal in London. Boats on the canal could be raised and lowered to different water levels.

Detective work

With an adult, visit a local canal. Some canals and bridges have the dates when they were built on plates or carved into the stone. Take rubbings of these.

The great waterway

Canals connected mines and factories. **Raw materials** could be transported to the places where they were needed. Canals also connected **ports** and large towns. This is so factory goods could be sold or shipped abroad.

Canal building began at the end of the eighteenth century. By 1860, there were more than 3,000 kilometres of canals in Britain. At this time, the railway began to take over from canals. It was quicker and cheaper to move heavy goods on trains.

A person remembers the wherries:

"...in those days they carried anything, people even, because it was the quickest way for people to get between Norwich and Yarmouth."

▲ *A Norfolk wherry.*

❧ Wherries had a mast that could be raised and lowered quickly. Why was this important?

▼ *Men building a canal.*

Sailing ships

In Victorian times, Britain led the world in trade and manufacturing. British ships carried raw materials and goods overseas. Ports, such as London and Liverpool, were centres of international trade.

Detective work

Find out what life was like on a Victorian ship. Visit your local library and look for old books containing descriptions of sea voyages.

People carriers

Large ships also carried millions of people to places such as America and Australia. Many poor people emigrated abroad. These **emigrants** were looking for new jobs and better homes. Their journeys were long and uncomfortable.

❧ Look at the picture of the emigrants on page 11. How do you think these people feel?

❧ Look for clues about where the emigrants below are going.

▼ *Irish emigrants wait at the dockside in Cork, Ireland.*

Iron ships

Ships got bigger and better in Victorian times. Iron **hulls** replaced wooden ones. These large ships had more masts, ropes and sails, too. They needed a large crew to sail them.

Clippers

Victorian 'clippers' were fast-sailing ships. They transported goods that went bad quickly, such as tea. Tea was grown in places such as India. At the start of the tea season, the first ships to reach Britain fetched the highest prices for their tea.

Steam ships

Steam ships eventually replaced clippers. They also took over the fastest cargo and passenger routes. However, sailing ships were still popular until after the First World War.

▲ What do you think this female emigrant has under her cape?

▼ Clippers were long, sleek ships that sped along the water.

How fast were steam ships?

Early steam ships had sails. The sails were used when the ship broke down or ran out of coal. In 1838, the British ship *Sirius* became the first boat to cross the Atlantic using only steam power. It took just 15 days to make the crossing. Sailing ships often took 40 days to do the same journey.

Powerful propellers

The first steam ships had wooden paddle wheels to drive them through the water. Eventually, new ships were fitted with metal **propellers**. These ships were much faster than those with paddle wheels.

▼ *The steam ship* British Queen *had a wooden paddle, which made her especially fast.*

▲ *The* Great Eastern *ship was eventually used to lay communication cables under the sea.*

Passenger boats

In 1854, the *Great Eastern* steam ship was launched. It was the largest ship ever built and could carry 4,000 passengers. It was slow compared to smaller ships. The *Great Eastern* was a good advert for British shipbuilding. By 1897, British companies were building half of the world's ships every year.

❧ Why did the *Great Eastern* have sails, paddle wheels and propellers?

❧ Why do you think the *Great Eastern* was slow?

▼ *These pleasure steamers on the River Thames are transporting people on day trips.*

Travelling by train

▲ *The third-class compartments on trains were overcrowded.*

The growth of the railways was probably the biggest change in transport. People believed that the railway was one of the greatest inventions of the age.

Steam trains

The first steam train was built by Richard Trevithick in 1804. It was heavy and kept breaking the rails. By 1837 trains had improved and Britain became gripped by 'railway mania'.

Passenger trains

At first, train passengers sat in open trucks. In time, coaches were covered and heated. There were three classes of travel. Third class travel was cheapest but the least comfortable.

Cheap travel

Poor Victorians could afford to use the trains. They used them for work and to go on day trips and holidays. Because it was easier to travel around, more people visited the seaside. Holiday resorts developed around the country.

Transporting food

Trains also meant that fresh food could be transported quickly. As a result, people had better diets.

Detective work

Find out more about the development of the railways. Visit a railway or transport museum. Look for advertisements for day trips and holidays. Use these to show the growth of the travel industry.

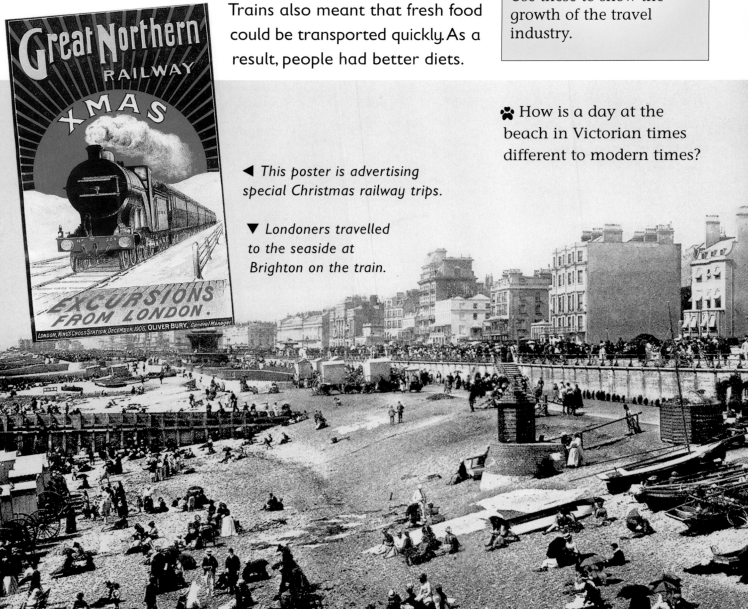

◀ This poster is advertising special Christmas railway trips.

▼ Londoners travelled to the seaside at Brighton on the train.

How is a day at the beach in Victorian times different to modern times?

The railway network

The first public train ran in 1825 on the Stockton and Darlington line. Other lines were soon opened. By 1901, the railway network covered many parts of the country.

A billion passengers

The railway network grew quickly. By 1837, there were 2,300 kilometres of track and by 1901, this had risen to 30,000 kilometres. One billion passengers used the trains each year.

◄ *An early steam train.*

Detective work

Try to find out when your local railway network was built. Local reference libraries may have county directories. These have details of when rail companies were founded and when stations were opened.

Building the network

Trains need to travel over level tracks so tunnels, **embankments** and bridges were built to keep the tracks as straight and level as possible. Stations, engine sheds, signal boxes and telegraph lines were also built for the trains.

Environmental damage

Some people were angry about the changes to the countryside. They also hated the pollution from trains. One person complained: 'Between Slough and Wycombe the country is poisoned by the foulest, the blackest, and the most sulphurous pest of smoke.'

▼ Building the Royal Albert Bridge in London.

▲ At Bath railway station, the arches are made of iron and glass.

✿ Why do you think the bridge was named after a member of the royal family?

Engineers and navvies

▲ *Isambard Kingdom Brunel.*

♣ What can you tell about Brunel from the portrait above?

The **engineers** who designed Britain's railways became national heroes. The men who built the railway network were called **navvies**. In their own way, they were heroes too.

The Great Western Railway

One of the most famous engineers was Isambard Kingdom Brunel. He designed the Great Western Railway. It ran from London to Bristol. He designed the track, bridges and tunnels. He even planned the railway buildings and carriages.

Unsung heroes

Navvies did not have machinery to help them build the railway network. Instead, they used shovels, pickaxes and gunpowder. Navvies could shift an average of 20 tonnes of rubble each day. They did not have helmets or safety equipment like workmen today. Many men were killed or injured on the job in falls, railway cave-ins and explosions.

◄ *The Clifton Suspension Bridge was designed by Brunel. It crosses a deep valley in Bristol.*

Bad behaviour

The navvies worked long hours. They lived in dirty, overcrowded huts. In their spare time, many of them drank and they often got into fights. This earned them a bad reputation and they were treated like villains rather than heroes.

Detective work

Look for biographies about other Victorian engineers, such as Robert Stephenson and Joseph Locke.

See if you can find stories about navvies in old newspapers.

▼ *These navvies are working on the railway line from London to the north of England.*

In 1846 Thomas Carlyle, a Scottish historian, said:

"All the roads and lanes are overrun with drunken navvies…"

Travelling around cities

▲ *Horse-drawn trams were used by people in cities.*

In 1833, a journalist described what it was like to travel on a horse omnibus:

"Here we all are…crammed and squeezed into each other like so many peas in a pod…"

❀ How is the experience described above like rush-hour travel today?

▶ *This tram is powered by steam so it goes faster than a horse-drawn tram.*

The first buses were carriages pulled by teams of horses. Later steam-powered buses were introduced to big cities such as Edinburgh and London. These buses were bigger and faster than horse-drawn carriages.

Omnibuses

The first buses were called omnibuses. The fares were so expensive that poor people could not afford to use them. Later, omnibuses became double-deckers. The seats on the top deck were cheaper but there was no protection from the weather.

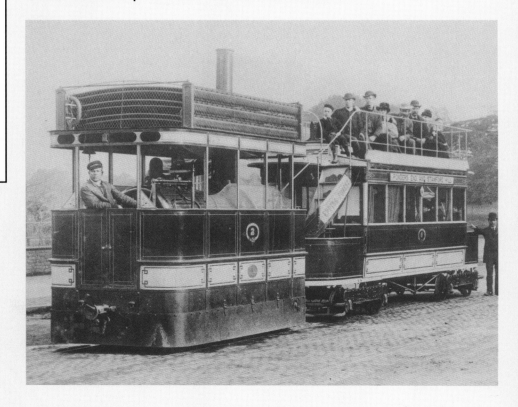

Horse-drawn trams

Trams looked like omnibuses but they ran on rails. The first trams were introduced in the 1860s. It was easier for the horses to pull carriages along rails than over bumpy streets. Trams could carry twice as many people as omnibuses using the same number of horses. They were popular because the fares were cheaper.

Steam and electricity

By 1885, some trams were powered by steam engines. These trams were quicker and cleaner than horse-drawn trams. Then in 1901, electric trams were introduced to some cities.

Detective work

Talk to older people about travelling on trams. Their experiences might be similar to those of the Victorians. Find out where the trams ran in your area in Victorian times.

◀ *Electric trams were seen as modern and stylish.*

Travelling underground

In 1863, the first underground railway was opened in London. People could escape the busy streets above and get to their destinations quickly.

Underground trains

The first underground trains were pulled by steam engines. The tunnels were so dark that passengers had to carry their own lamps or candles. The trains also filled with smoke and steam. In the 1890s, electric trains came into use. They had their own lights. Underground travel became cleaner and much more enjoyable.

▲ *What kinds of transport can you see in this photograph?*

▼ *These workers are building tunnels for underground trains in London.*

❧ How are the tunnels in this picture being built? (See page 23 to find out more)

Trains on cables

In 1896, the Glasgow Underground network was opened. It was different from the London Underground because the trains were connected to moving cables, which pulled the carriages along. When the driver wanted to stop the train, he had to disconnect the train from the cable.

Detective work

Find maps of Victorian underground railway systems at transport museums, underground companies and Record Offices. Compare the old maps to modern maps of the underground.

▲ *Visitors tour the London Underground.*

In 1866, one London Underground traveller complained:

"...the darkness of the tunnels, the heat of the gas-lighted carriages in the summer... and the fear of unknown ... dangers."

Building tunnels

Early underground tunnels were made using the 'cut-and-cover' method. Large tunnels were dug. Then, the walls and roof of the tunnels were built. Finally, earth was piled on top of the tunnels. Later, engineers invented a better method. They found a way to tunnel through the ground and put large metal tubes underground.

Bicycles

'You have heard of old Pegasus flying no doubt
But our Hobbies now Beat him good lack
For when you are tired of Riding about
You may Carry your Horse on your Back

▲ *This cartoon shows the dangers of riding a 'hobby horse' bicycle.*

▼ *Another early bicycle was called the penny-farthing.*

The first bicycles were invented before Victorian times. They were like scooters with seats. They were called 'hobby horses'.

Pedal bicycles

The first bicycle with pedals was invented in 1839, but cycling did not become popular until the 1860s. One early type of bicycle was nicknamed the **boneshaker** because it was so uncomfortable to ride.

The American author Mark Twain wrote about bicycles in the 1880s:

"Get a bicycle. You will not regret it if you live."

Why do you think that some Victorians wanted women cyclists to be banned?

◄ *Women wore trousers so that they could ride their bicycles.*

Detective Work

Contact local cycle clubs for information about Victorian bicycles. Then, draw a cartoon strip or a time line showing the different kinds of bicycle of the time.

The cycling craze

In 1885, James Starley invented the 'safety' bicycle. It had brakes and a chain attached to the back wheel. In 1888, tyres that were filled with air were added.

Cycling soon became fashionable. Cycle clubs were set up all over the country and members got together for tours and picnics. Bicycle racing on special tracks also caught on. Cycling contests were included in the first modern Olympic games in Greece in 1896.

Cheap transport

Bicycles were not just for fun. Poor Victorians used them to travel to work. Many shops and small businesses used bicycles for making deliveries to their customers.

Early cars

◀ A Benz motorcar built in 1888.

❀ Many early cars had three wheels. Why do you think four-wheel cars were more popular?

The first cars were invented at the end of the nineteenth century. They were known as 'horseless carriages'. The word 'carriage' was shortened to car.

The first cars

At first, cars had steam engines. These cars were heavy and difficult to drive. A German called Karl Benz designed a petrol engine car in 1885. It was the first car to go on sale to the public. British companies were soon making petrol-engine cars, too. These early cars were very slow so it was still quicker to travel by horse.

Dirty and dangerous

Early cars were noisy, dirty and broke down a lot. Passengers rode in the open so they had to wrap up warmly. Drivers needed **goggles** to protect their eyes. Many people thought cars were dangerous. Until 1896, cars were only allowed to travel at walking pace behind a man carrying a red flag.

For the rich

Only the rich could afford to buy cars in the early days of motoring. Cars became more popular after Queen Victoria's reign.

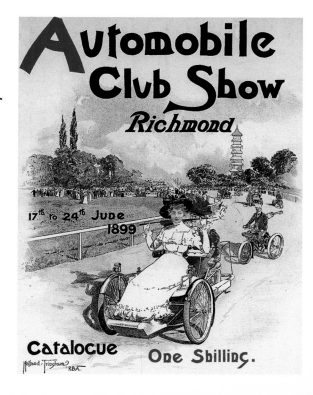

Detective work

Find newspapers from the 1890s in your local Record Office or library. Look for stories and adverts for cars.

▲ The Automobile Club was started in 1897. Car owners could become members. The club organised races and shows for its members.

▼ Passengers in cars needed warm, waterproof clothes.

Your project

If you have been following the paw-prints in this book you should have plenty of clues about Victorian transport. These clues will help you with your project.

Topic Questions

- *How did travel improve in Victorian times?*

- *What effect did the railways have on Britain?*

- *How was travel different for rich and poor people?*

- *How did ships change during Queen Victoria's reign?*

- *What jobs did Victorian transport workers do?*

▼ *The West India Docks, London, in 1895.*

▲ A steam train at Paddington Station, London, in 1892.

Think of ways to present your project. These ideas may help you:

- Write a Victorian diary. Describe the different ways of travelling.

- Make a Victorian newspaper. This could include stories and adverts for travel.

- Produce a Victorian holiday brochure. Describe the kinds of transport on offer.

▼ A first-class carriage on a Victorian train was luxurious.

Shelock Bones on the case...

You may find an unusual subject for your project. Sherlock Bones found out how better transport systems helped to improve the postal service.

Glossary

barge A flat-bottomed boat used for moving goods on canals and rivers.

boneshaker A nickname for early Victorian bicycles with solid tyres.

canals Waterways that have been built by people.

embankment A long, low earth or stone bank built to carry a railway.

emigrant Someone that goes to live in another country.

empire Countries and land overseas ruled by another country.

engineer Someone who is trained to design and build machines, roads, bridges and railways.

goggles Special glasses made to protect the eyes from dust and dirt.

hull The main body or frame of a ship.

lock Part of a canal that is closed off by gates. The gates can be opened and shut to release or hold water in. This means the water level can be raised and lowered to let boats pass through.

manufacturer A business where things are made with machines, such as a factory.

navvies Workers who dug canals and railways. Navvy is short for navigator.

port A place where ships can load and unload goods.

propeller A set of blades that turns at high speed. This creates enough force to push a boat through the water.

raw materials The basic things used to make something, such as coal, wood and iron ore.

telegraph A way of sending messages by electric current.

Answers

Page 5

❧ The picture shows three forms of transport – horse and cart, steam train and travelling by foot.

Page 6

❧ There are 13 people in the stagecoach, including the driver and people inside the carriage.

Page 9

❧ Wherries had masts that were easy to lower because of the many low bridges on canals they needed to pass under.

Page 10

❧ These people were probably feeling scared and seasick.
❧ There are signs for Quebec in Canada and Boston and New York in America.

Page 11

❧ The woman has a baby under her cape.

Page 13

❧ The *Great Eastern* had sails, paddle wheels and propellers because nobody knew how well the paddle wheels and propellers would work.
❧ The *Great Eastern* was a heavy ship and it carried a lot of coal for the journey so it was slow.

Page 15

❧ The people in the photograph are wearing more clothes than people would wear today. Victorians did not approve showing their bodies in public.

Page 17

Bridges, buildings and streets were often named after the royal family because the royals were important to the country.

Page 18

Brunel is shown with many books so he was very clever and studied hard.

Page 20

Travelling in rush-hour traffic today can be cramped and unpleasant, just like in the Victorian times. Transport has improved these days but there are far more passengers.

Page 22

The tunnels in this picture are being built using the 'cut-and-cover' method.

Page 25

Many people thought that women who took exercise were 'common' and 'unladylike'.

Page 26

Four-wheeled cars were better than three-wheeled cars on rough roads because they were sturdier. They were also faster.

Books to read

Victorian Life: Transport by Nicola Barber (Wayland, 2008)

Victorian Flashbacks: The Voyage of the 'Silver Bream' by Theresa Tomlinson (A&C Black, 2002)

Sparks: Kidnap on the Canal by George Buchanan (Franklin Watts, 2000)

Places to visit

London Transport Museum
www.ltmuseum.co.uk

National Maritime Museum
www.nmm.ac.uk

National Railway Museum
www.nrm.org.uk

Index